❝ This part of the world was the heartbeat of the survival of this country. Without our gentlemen and ladies, we would not have survived those dark years... Winston Churchill said we were within two weeks of losing the war, but the ladies and gentlemen of Liverpool and elsewhere did it for this country. **❞**

Canon Bob Evans, former head of the Mersey Mission to Seamen

A ship convoy on its way sailing
through the North Sea in March 1943

CONTENTS

Written by Peter Elson, Vicky Andrews,
Chris Brereton, Catherine Jones, David Charters
Design & Production: Vicky Andrews
Cover Design: Colin Harrison, Rick Cooke

Liverpool Post & ECHO image archive:
Brian Johnston, Mike Price, Colin Lane,
James Maloney, Jason Roberts
Pictures courtesy of the
Liverpool Post and Echo,
Mirrorpix, Royal Navy

With thanks to National Museums Liverpool,
Liverpool Western Approaches Museum,
The National Archives

Contact us: lostliverpool@trinitymirror.com

Trinity Mirror Media

Managing Director: Ken Rogers
Senior Editor: Steve Hanrahan
Editor: Paul Dove
Senior Art Editor: Rick Cooke
Senior Marketing Executive: Claire Brown
Sales and Marketing Manager: Elizabeth Morgan
Sales and Marketing Assistant: Karen Cadman
Advertising: Paul Ritson 0151 239 5918

Printed by PCP

ISBN 9781908695475

EYE OF THE STORM

Crucial role of Liverpool in the Battle of Atlantic is recognised for the 70th anniversary

IT was long, agonising, bloody and the only conflict of the Second World War which prime minister Winston Churchill said kept him awake at night.

But even so, that must have accounted for an awful lot of sleepless nights as the Battle of the Atlantic raged - or simply ground on relentlessly - for the entire span of the war from September 3, 1939, to May 8, 1945.

Widely regarded as the "longest, largest and most complex" naval battle in history, thousands of ships were drawn into more than 100 convoy battles with 1,000 single ship engagements over a theatre of war spread across thousands of hostile square miles of ocean.

Without the extreme courage, dedication and ingenuity of men and women from all walks of life both the Battle of the Atlantic and the war itself would have been much shorter with Britain forced to surrender to Germany.

As an island nation dependent on imports, our merchant fleet could have been crushed by Kriegsmarine (German Navy) and the country starved into early submission to Adolf Hitler's Nazi regime.

Winning the Battle of the Atlantic to keep the supply lines open from North America and the Caribbean was as important to this nation's survival as had been the Battle of Britain in 1940.

Yet while the land battle barely started in the first year (a period dubbed the 'phoney war'), it began at sea within 12 hours and Liverpool was immediately in the front-line.

Without warning, the passenger liner SS Athenia was torpedoed and sunk by a German U-boat, out-bound from Liverpool to Canada with the loss of 117 men, women and children.

However this was merely a curtain-raiser as Britain and its Allies announced a naval blockade of Germany the day after the declaration of war and Germany responded in kind.

In less than a year of Athenia's loss, the Battle of the Atlantic was at its height in mid-1940.

Britain was swept into a deadly struggle for food and freedom. It made Liverpool central to the Allies' defiance of Nazi Germany – and therefore a prime Luftwaffe (the German airforce) bombing target.

The intensity of the Blitzkrieg on Liverpool's Home Front was also provoked as the Luftwaffe attempted to annihilate the top secret Western Approaches command and operational centre ("the Citadel") at Derby House, from which Allied forces in the Battle of the Atlantic were controlled around the clock from 1941. ➤

BATTLE of the ATLANTIC · 70th ANNIVERSARY

BOA70

The famous statue showing Captain Frederic 'Johnnie' Walker looking out to sea at Liverpool Pier Head is a fitting tribute to the Battle of the Atlantic

RMS Athenia was the first British ship to be sunk by Nazi Germany in World War II – she was torpedoed without warning west of Scotland by the German submarine U-30

A torpedo from a U-boat had cut this ship practically in two, August 1941

➤ The convoys gathered largely in Halifax, Nova Scotia, Canada, to make the perilous voyage across the U-boat infested North Atlantic to Liverpool.

Meantime, the Arctic Convoys, composed of many Merseyside ships and seafarers, left Liverpool destined for Murmansk, in Soviet Russia, sailing through appalling sub-zero conditions.

Although convoys were the best system to protect merchant ships from U-boats hunting in wolf-packs and alone, the losses of ships and crews were horrendous.

Throughout 1942, the destruction of Allied shipping was done with great efficiency in the "Second Happy Time", by the German Admiral Karl Doenitz's U-boats to the "Black May" of 1943.

The Battle of the Atlantic saw Doenitz's U-boats, backed by German warships and the Luftwaffe in deadly conflict with the Royal Navy, Royal Canadian Navy, the British Merchant Navy aided by our allies.

"Besides the nightmare of the U-boat menace, this Battle running for the duration of the war, was fought in a cold almost too terrible to imagine," said David Charters, Merseyside writer and historian.

"The drips on the ends of men's noses would turn to ice and naked hands could freeze to the rails of ships carrying vital supplies to Britain.

"All that suffering is just reduced to those words, Battle of the Atlantic."

By the end of March 1943, the number of ships lost had been drastically reduced. While the worst crisis was over by the end

of 1943, the Battle of the Atlantic continued and the North Atlantic and elsewhere remained dangerous for Allied shipping. Our ships kept the sea lanes open between North America and Britain in the build-up to the Normandy landings and the invasion of Europe.

It should not be forgotten that for the entire war U-boat production never ceased and was bolstered by Japanese and Italian submarines.

Even with only four months of war to go, 30 U-boats were launched in 1945. By then the Germans had created very impressive submarines, with longer cruising ranges and higher speeds. These were the ocean-going Type XXI of 1,600 tons and the coastal Type XXIII of 230 tons.

Incredibly, by March, 1945, when Nazi Germany was crumbling before the Allied in the west and the Russians in the east, the U-boat fleet achieved its zenith of 463 vessels.

Thankfully, it had limited opportunities to exercise its new power, boxed in by the Allied navies.

But even as U-boat fired the first shots of the war, so it ended it by torpedoing a Norwegian freighter in the English Channel on the penultimate day of the war.

Andrew Williams, who produced a definitive BBC documentary series on the Battle of the Atlantic and a novel, The Interrogator, set in the conflict, feels very strongly we should not forget.

"The public still do not understand how important it was, as it was all fought out at sea beyond everyone's eyes," he said.

"Yet in Merseyside alone so many were killed and so much devastated.

"Newspaper reports were restricted and no-one saw what was lost; ships came in and left and some never came back.

"Unlike the Battle of Britain, D-Day or Dunkirk, it was a very unknown part of the conflict and we don't give it full weight."

David Charters adds: "The veterans of this great battle will never march together again in Liverpool.

"But that does not mean their sacrifice, their courage, their skill and dedication should ever be forgotten.

"The city's waterfront will always be their spiritual home, a resting place for the spirits of the men and women who answered their country's call in its darkest days."

An anti-U-boat depth charge crew get ready to drop some charges, April 1941

On the deck of the US Coast Guard cutter Spencer, watching the explosion of a depth charge which blasted U-175's hope of breaking into the centre of a large convoy, 1943

War diaries of Admiral Horton

TAKEN from the war diaries of Admiral Sir Max Horton, Commander in Chief, Western Approaches, in March 1943:

This period had witnessed the greatest effort yet made by U-boats on both Trans-Atlantic and Southbound convoys. Losses in convoy are considerably greater than for any similar period, but serious as these losses are there are two outstanding features in our favour to set against them.

(a) Despite large "pack" attacks in some of which the enemy doubtless hoped to muster 20 U-boats, no convoy has been dispersed and annihilated.

(b) The enemy has only averaged the sinking of 1 ship per U-boat on patrol for a month and this must seem a poor return for a concentrated major effort against the Allied Nation's principle supply line.

2. There are however factors which offer encouragement for the future:—

(a) An improvement in the weather conditions at this time of the year should increase the number of effective vessels in each group.

(b) The appointment of a Training Captain to HMS Philante is being followed by an intensive training drive for all groups.

(c) More escort oilers are coming into service and with an improvement in their equipment, the operation of fuelling at sea should be greatly facilitated.

(d) It is hoped to operate support groups in the near future.

(e) The provision of Very-Long-Range aircraft is being speeded up.

(f) It is hoped to operate escort carriers on the North Atlantic Convoy routes in the near future.

3. The following convoys were attacked during this period:—

HX 227 March 1 — one straggler sunk in 50° 29'N, 35° 26W.

XK 2 March 5 — 4 ships sunk in 44°N, 15°W.

ON 170 March 9 — 1 ship sunk in 61° 34'N, 27° 43'W.

OS 44 March 13 — 4 ships sunk in 42° 45'N, 13° 50'W.

4. The two heaviest attacks however were directed against SC 121 and HX 228. In the former case up to 16 U-boats may have been operating for 5 days against SC 121. 6 ships in convoy and 1 straggler were sunk and 5 ships missing must be presumed sunk. In the case of HX 228 up to 6 U-boats may well have been operating over 3 days. 5 ships were sunk — Against this Harvester rammed and sank U-444 — 5 prisoners, but herself was torpedoed later by U-432 which in turn was sunk by the Free French Corvette Aconit.

5. There were several other promising attacks both by aircraft and surface vessels.

A huge crowd cheers HMS Magpie home to Liverpool after the record-breaking anti-U-boat patrol in February 1944, with other sloops in the 2nd Support Group, including Capt Johnnie Walker and HMS Starling, following into Gladstone Dock

"The only thing that ever really frightened me during the war was the U-boat peril."
Winston Churchill

The aftermath of the Blitz – the Queen Victoria monument remains intact but the scene from Derby Square is one of total devastation

IN THE LINE OF FIRE

Liverpool's finest hour and her greatest sacrifice...

IT is impossible to over-estimate the importance of Merseyside during World War II.

Millions of tons of food, materials, fuel and military equipment needed to be shipped in to Liverpool to feed, clothe and defend her people. It was left to the courageous merchant seamen, and the navies who protected them, to keep open those channels to the Americas, Africa and beyond.

The area was the headquarters for the relentless war against the U-boats, the main gateway to Britain for millions of tons of food and war materials, and an essential naval repair base.

It also played a leading part in the invasion of North Africa, the liberation of Malta, and the D-Day landings. And it offered a friendly face for thousands of sailors who poured in on shore leave. Day and night the Port of Liverpool's army of 50,000 workers toiled for the war effort. Between 1939 and 1945, they dealt with 1,285 convoys.

All this made the city a target. And it paid the price. More than 10,000 people died or were injured, and docks and homes on both sides of the Mersey were devastated. Houses, hospitals, churches and shops all bore the brunt of the bombing.

Liverpool's biggest docks are actually located in Bootle, making the north Liverpool borough the central port in the Battle of the Atlantic in terms of its size.

As the main docks for receiving vital ammunition and materials from the US, Canada and the West Indies, it suffered very heavy bombing. Another reason was Bootle being base for the convoy escort groups led by the ace Battle of the Atlantic commanders, Captains Johnnie Walker, Peter Gretton and Donald McIntyre.

Between August 1940 and October 1941, 1,886 people were killed or injured in Bootle. In one night on May 3-4 1941 it was bombed continuously for three-and-a-half hours.

Bootle Town Hall is a repository of fascinating mementos of this time, including bizarre artefacts like the Bedford Road Infants school clock, which stopped at 11.34pm - the exact time an incendiary bomb exploded there.

Brunswick Street, from the junction with Fenwick Street. The ruins of the Corn Exchange are on the left, the rear of India Buildings are on the right.

Surveying the damage caused by the air raid bombs in Liverpool

Above, a major search, rescue and clean-up operation is underway in a number of areas on Lace Street, near Byrom Street, Scotland Road. Bottom picture, pedestrians carry on with their business at the junction of Ranelagh Street, Renshaw Street and Lime Street, with the burnt-out shell of Lewis's department store, left

Civilians walk under damaged power lines after an air raid in Liverpool, the city centre reduced to a smouldering ruin

Liverpool has stood up enormously well to its task... we still have that unshaken belief in the ultimate victory.

Lord Mayor of Liverpool, Alderman Sir Sydney Jones, 1941

Members of the
Liverpool company of
the Girls' Training Corps
visit a gun site manned
by Ack-Ack women,
September 1942

Above, a Dutch troopship arrives in Liverpool with repatriated prisoners of war from Malaya, October 1945, after the war's end

American soldiers play baseball amid the ruins in the business centre of Liverpool, circa 1943

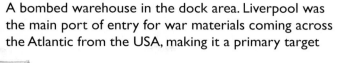

A bombed warehouse in the dock area. Liverpool was the main port of entry for war materials coming across the Atlantic from the USA, making it a primary target

The bombed out remains of administration buildings and warehouses in the Liverpool docks following an air raid by the Luftwaffe during the blitz

Left, the scene in Water Street, Liverpool, in 1939, 17 days after war was declared. The lines of sandbags form part of an air raid defence system. The Town Hall is pictured right, and nearby, Derby House – the building which was later to be become the combined headquarters for the Battle of the Atlantic

Winston Churchill addresses dockers and seamen during a visit to the North West in April 1941, commending them for their contribution to the Battle of the Atlantic. The censor has removed the location but it is thought to have been in Liverpool during the Blitz.

U-BOAT HUNTERS BENEATH THE CITY

Chris Brereton discovers a museum dedicated to the frontline of the battle in Liverpool...

IF you walk up Chapel Street in Liverpool - away from the fabled waterfront and home to the statue of legendary U-boat hunter Captain Johnnie Walker - and turn right onto Rumford Street, you come to an off-white building that looks much the same as others in the city's Business District.

However, Derby House, at Exchange Flags, is far more than just another office block.

In fact Derby House can lay claim to being the most vital building in the entire history of the Battle of the Atlantic.

For it was within these cavernous surroundings that Western Approaches, the Allied's Combined Operations unit, was housed from February 1941 until the end of World War Two in 1945. The Allies' early response to the German naval threat was co-ordinated from

Plymouth until it was decided to move it to Liverpool as the city was Britain's most crucial convoy port, receiving around 1,000 ships a week piled high with vital war equipment and supplies.

Renovations to Derby House made it bomb proof and gas proof and the building was reinforced with a seven-foot thick roof and three-foot thick walls. ➤

Inside the Western Approach museum in Liverpool's city centre. The main wall charts are in the Operations Room at the former top secret HQ, hidden underneath Exchange Flags

World War II operations centre in Derby House

➤ The message was clear: bomb us if you like – but nothing will stop the Allies from fighting hard in the Atlantic.

At any one time, 200 members of staff – mostly WRENs and WAAFs – were working inside the building, plotting the whereabouts of Allied convoys as well and co-ordinating the RAF and Royal Navy's response to the threat from the dreaded German U-boats.

The 55,000 square foot building had sleeping quarters, secret transmission rooms – with an armed guard outside at all times – and even a direct line to the Cabinet in Downing Street in case Prime Minister Winston Churchill needed to be informed quickly of developments out on the Atlantic.

Visitors to Western Approaches, which first opened as a museum in May 1993, take a winding pathway down into the building's basement where they get a glimpse into a forgotten world of morse code, teleprinters and telegrams.

They may look primitive to the modern eye but Western Approaches was at the very cutting edge of technology for the time.

Information constantly poured into the main Operations Room – equipped with an enormous map on one wall – and plotters would then move models on and around the map to show the progress of a convoy or indicate where and when an Allied attack was taking place on the enemy.

The Flag Officer on duty would oversee this hub of activity and report to his superiors on events out on the stormy sea, where the deadliest game of cat and mouse there has ever been was underway 24 hours a day.

70 years may have passed since Derby House's finest hour but the passage of time has done little to diminish the sense of awe visitors can feel when exploring this underground strategy room.

World War Two was principally won by brave men fighting on land, sea and in the air.

But it was also won by places like Western Approaches, by unassuming, unsung heroes co-ordinating and communicating in order to give the Allies' convoys and naval forces every possible chance of emerging unscathed.

Margaret Jones, the museum's curator underlines exactly how vital the role played by Western Approaches was.

"If the Allies had lost the Battle of the Atlantic, they would almost certainly have lost the war," she said.

Constant radio contact was maintained with the sea force and the HQ based off Chapel Street throughout the operation

"And they wouldn't have won the Battle of the Atlantic without Western Approaches. It really is that simple.

"The building's importance should never be forgotten or underestimated and it is important to remind both present and future generations of its significance."

So next time you walk up Chapel Street in Liverpool – away from the fabled waterfront and home to the statue of legendary U-boat hunter Captain Johnnie Walker – and you turn right onto Rumford Street, spend some time in the off-white building that looks much the same as others in the city's Business District.

And give thanks to the men and women who worked inside it 24 hours a day to ensure the Battle of the Atlantic ended in victory.

A Royal Air Force Coastal Command Sunderland flying boat protects a Union Castle Line troopship in the Atlantic in 1941

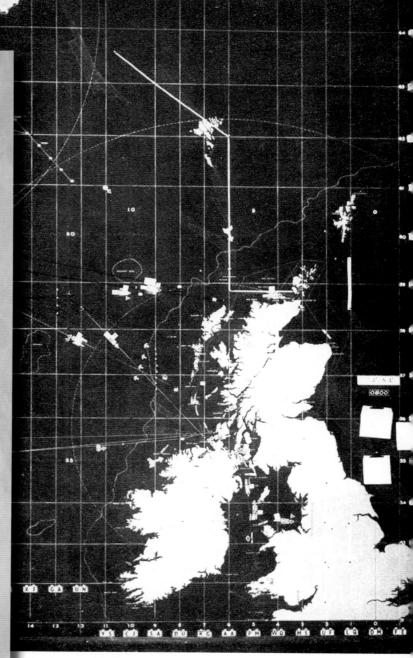

Secret bunker

KNOWING that another world war was approaching, Winston Churchill, then First Lord of the Admiralty, while on a visit to Liverpool in the late 1930s, ordered a top secret command bunker to be built beneath Derby House, at Exchange Flags.

The Western Approaches combined operations centre (Royal Navy, Royal Marines and RAF), was a wartime command centre containing a 100 rooms and able to withstand 500lb bombs – the biggest at the time.

Opening in 1941, it was populated by hundreds of officers, Wrens and Waafs, day and night, who were guarded round the clock by Royal Marines. It contained the world's first anti-submarine school, in which Prince Philip trained for two courses of three week.

After its highly successful role in overseeing the Battle of the Atlantic, closure came in August 1945, and it was left to quietly moulder away. Entirely forgotten, the empty bunker would indeed have been lost except for the determination of one man, Fred O'Brien, whose vision ensured its revival as a museum and memorial to those who served there and at sea.

"It is the most socially worthwhile thing I have ever done, in spite of all the trials and tribulations setting it up," said Fred.

As a teenager, Fred was intrigued as the Liverpool Cathedral tomb of former Western Approaches' commander-in-chief, Admiral Sir Max Horton.

"Over the years I researched Western Approaches and the Battle of the Atlantic and realised it is as important as the signing of the Magna Carta," said Fred, a retired architect and designer.

"Tactics devised by Admiral Max Horton and Captain Johnnie Walker, plus new technology, turned the tide for Britain and Allies in 1943.

"In December 1988, I read in the Echo that the property developer Bill Davis' Walton Group had acquired Derby House. I convinced him the bunker should be opened up. There's no natural light and it's unsuitable for any other use.

"The project director James Fox sourced all sorts of authentic equipment to refurbish the rooms. We opened it on May 27, 1993, to coincide with the Battle of the Atlantic 50th anniversary.

"It's great to see it is still there and open to the public."

> **"This was where the Battle of the Atlantic was won..."**
>
> *Horst Bredow, Head of U-Boat Archive, Germany, on a visit to Western Approaches*

Top left, one of the morale-boosting posters inside Derby House; top right, the white Ensign of this warship had seen better days during the Battle of the Atlantic; below, captain and his crew keep watch from the bridge of a ship in an Atlantic convoy in 1940

Plotting the convoys and docks at Derby House

Exhibitions inside the museum, beneath Liverpool's Exchange Flags, include the combined main switchboard room, a bust in memory of Captain Johnnie Walker, the canteen, and the switchboard control rack

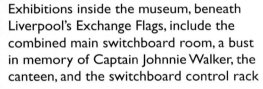

King George VI and Queen Elizabeth visiting Derby House, Liverpool in June 1945

DURING THE BATTLE OF THE ATLANTIC IN THE SECOND WORLD WAR COMBINED HEADQUARTERS WESTERN APPROACHES WAS SITUATED IN THIS BUILDING 1941–1945

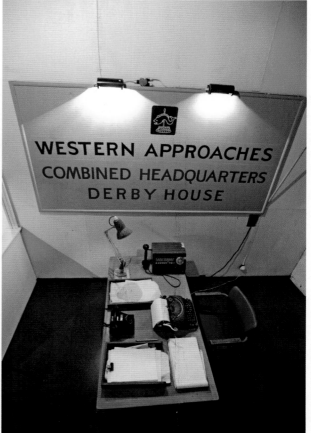

WESTERN APPROACHES COMBINED HEADQUARTERS DERBY HOUSE

EMERGENCY POWER BOARD

Writer whose love of the city was forged in the nightmare of war

THE dreadful wail of the air raid siren remained inextricably connected to Elizabeth Elgin's bittersweet memories of Liverpool.

As a teenage Wren, she spent her waking hours in the bowels of Derby House, working in the teleprinter room.

Between shaking uncontrollably each time a siren was sounded and enjoying her new found freedom, Betty, as she preferred to be known, was unconsciously gathering material for her future novels. Many of them would be set in war ravaged Liverpool or feature local women.

On her time working in Derby House, Betty recalled: "I was not allowed to roam everywhere during the war. There were ID cards which were colour coded and the only place I was allowed to go was in Communications. If I tried to go anywhere else there would be a big burly man at the door to stop me.

"There was three feet of reinforced concrete above us but they forgot to put air conditioning in. It was very, very noisy when the printers were all clattering, you had to shut your ears to it. And they generated their own heat too.

"One of the things I really remember is that we had all these black teleprinters but there was one special grey one. That was the direct line to Washington. Only good operators could use it because you had to send the message and then shut it down quickly or the Germans could have found the cable. I was a good operator and worked on it.

"What I sent in Liverpool came out in another world."

Betty met her husband, George, on a submarine depot ship when he told her off for whistling on board. They married in May, 1944 and scraped together enough money to buy a small house in Mulberry Road, Tuebrook, after the war.

It wasn't until 1989 that Betty began writing her first book, a war novel called All The Sweet Memories, about three Wrens stationed in Liverpool.

In all, she completed over 20 best-selling novels. When George retired, the couple moved to the Vale of York, the small village where Betty was born. She lived there until her death in 2005.

Author Betty Elgin pictured during her time as a wren in Derby House

"Hold your heads high by virtue of a double qualification – that of having served in the Navy, or Air Force and that of having taken part in the Battle of the Atlantic.**"**

Admiral Sir Max Horton

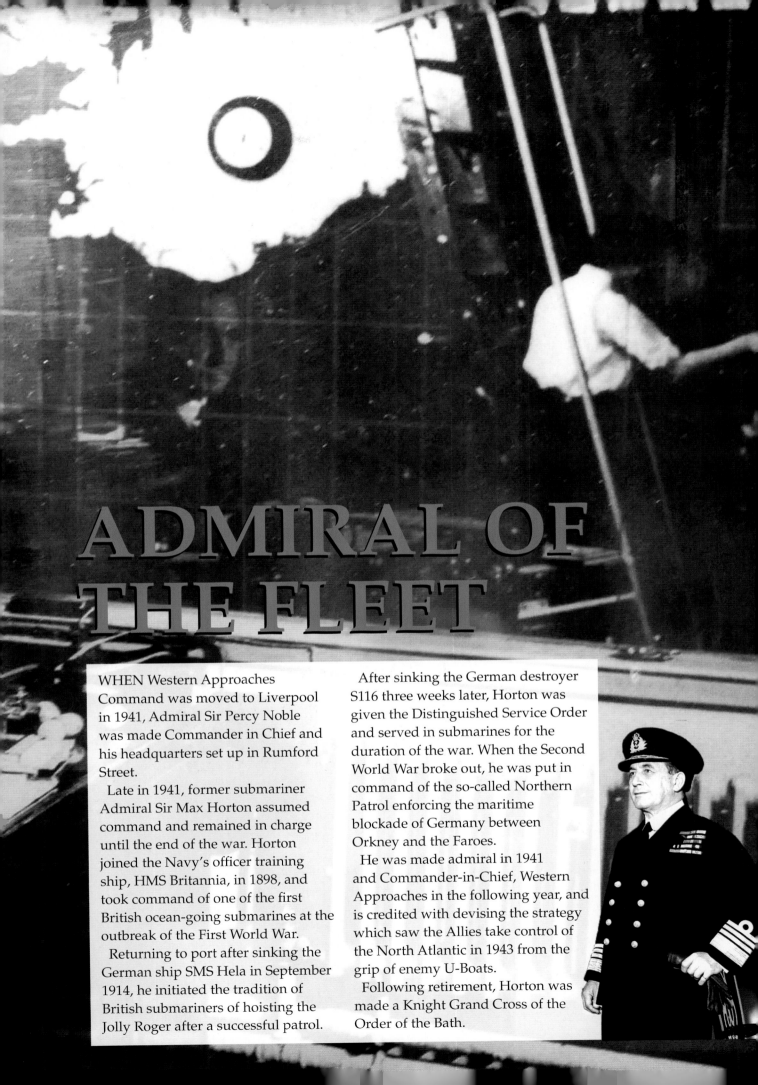

ADMIRAL OF THE FLEET

WHEN Western Approaches Command was moved to Liverpool in 1941, Admiral Sir Percy Noble was made Commander in Chief and his headquarters set up in Rumford Street.

Late in 1941, former submariner Admiral Sir Max Horton assumed command and remained in charge until the end of the war. Horton joined the Navy's officer training ship, HMS Britannia, in 1898, and took command of one of the first British ocean-going submarines at the outbreak of the First World War.

Returning to port after sinking the German ship SMS Hela in September 1914, he initiated the tradition of British submariners of hoisting the Jolly Roger after a successful patrol.

After sinking the German destroyer S116 three weeks later, Horton was given the Distinguished Service Order and served in submarines for the duration of the war. When the Second World War broke out, he was put in command of the so-called Northern Patrol enforcing the maritime blockade of Germany between Orkney and the Faroes.

He was made admiral in 1941 and Commander-in-Chief, Western Approaches in the following year, and is credited with devising the strategy which saw the Allies take control of the North Atlantic in 1943 from the grip of enemy U-Boats.

Following retirement, Horton was made a Knight Grand Cross of the Order of the Bath.

HERO OF THE OCEAN

No single naval personality embodied the Battle of the Atlantic spirit of courage, daring and self-sacrifice than that of Captain Johnnie Walker

CAPTAIN Frederic "Johnnie" Walker was one of the greatest naval heroes this country has ever known and hailed as "U-boat Killer Number One".

Thankfully for all of us, it was a case of "cometh the hour, cometh the man".

Ironically, in spite of his later phenomenal wartime success, the charismatic Capt Walker was not always perceived to be a navy high flyer.

Born in 1896, Frederic John Walker joined the Royal Navy as a 13-year-old. However, he passed out top of his class at Dartmouth and received the King's Medal.

He fought in the First World War and, aged just 21, became involved in the battle against U-boats that was to dominate his career. Walker was one of the first volunteers to study on specialist courses at the newly-formed anti-submarine school at Portland, in Dorset. By 1926, he was Fleet Anti-Submarine Officer in the Atlantic and Mediterranean Fleets. But his field of expertise was not then fashionable, with a trend was towards bigger and better surface ships with huge

artillery firepower. But as the Battle of the Atlantic spun out of Allied control from July 1940 to April 1941, in a period dubbed "Happy Time" by the U-boat crews, Walker came to the attention of Commander in Chief of the Western Approaches, Admiral Sir Percy Noble, and in 1941 given command of the sloop HMS Stork as senior officer of the 36th Escort Group.

While Walker and his family moved into Grassendale Park, Aigburth, on the banks of the Mersey, his escort group's home was Bootle's Gladstone Dock and its first success came in December 1941 with the protection of convoy HG-76.

This was Walker's chance to prove his theory that the battle should be taken to the enemy, with the offensive use of air and sea forces giving the best chance of doing maximum damage to U-boats while continuing to protect convoys.

At least seven U-boats were destroyed by Capt Walker before he left Stork on his appointment as Captain (D), Liverpool, in June 1942.

The hunt is on in this dramatic bridge scene on board the Starling, as Captain Walker, his right hand cluthing a hastily grabbed sandwich, takes a bearing on a submerged U-boat on receiving a report: "Echo 180 degrees, 2000 yards Sir"

Merseyside came to know this brilliant natural leader well in his new shore post as the escort groups' administrator.

However, in 1942 alone, 1,664 Allied ships totalling almost eight million tons were lost, the great majority due to U-boat attacks. While Britain and the Allies were being pummelled on this scale, the invasion of Europe could not be contemplated.

Because of this, the gentlemanly Noble was replaced by the tougher Sir Max Horton, who took over as C-in-C at the Western Approaches command bunker, beneath Derby House, Liverpool, dubbed "The Citadel".

Admiral Horton was a First World War submarine commander and his knowledge of this particular warfare led to a new strategy. More destroyers and frigates were needed to chase, harry and destroy the U-boats.

By now Walker was badgering the Admiralty to let him "stop sailing a desk" and go back to sea. ➤

Kathy Townsend, of Burscough, an RN nurse who helped care for Captain Walker in his final illness

HMS Starling drops one of 200 depth charges on U-264 in the Western Approaches in February 1944

➤ As a superlative sailor, Walker was the ideal man to carry out Horton's advanced strategy and turn the hunters into the hunted.

February 1943 saw Walker get his wish with command of the newly-built HMS Starling. Half of his old crew from HMS Stork joined him.

The 46-year-old took overall command of the 2nd Support Group comprising escort warships HMSs Wild Goose, Wren, Kite, Cygnet and Woodpecker.

The basic theory was to send the escort warships ahead of their convoys and force the U-boats wolf-packs underwater so they could not torpedo the merchant ships, but could be depth-charged.

The success of this strategy made his name synonymous with the spirit that helped win the Battle of the Atlantic. He hunted down 25 U-boats and urged his 2nd Support Group on to other "kills", often through a loudspeaker on his flag ships HMS Stork and later HMS Starling.

In one dramatic offensive, when three U-boats were destroyed, Walker hoisted the historic signal "General Chase", which had been used only twice before: once by Sir Francis Drake when he sighted the Spanish Armada.

He often hunted his victims well away from the merchant ship convoys. On one trip two U-boats were sunk 40 miles away from the convoy. On another occasion, he hunted U-202 to exhaustion over 14 hours.

But it was also the increasingly exhausted Walker who faced a premature end as his battle against the U-boats came at a heavy cost.

After returning from the Operation Neptune patrol, he collapsed from cerebral thrombosis during a visit with his wife Eileen to a Liverpool cinema, on July 7, 1944.

Two days later he died in Seaforth Naval Hospital. He was just 47.

His naval record was second to none, with 25 1/2 U-boat kills credited to him, the half being shared by the RAF.

His legacy are brilliant, far-seeing concepts for anti-submarine training.

The funeral itself was almost akin to a state funeral. Such was his renown that the Admiralty pronounced: "Captain Frederic John Walker more than any other won the Battle of the Atlantic.

"His methods had amazing success and, more than any other factor, gave the Royal Navy supremacy. No tribute could be too high for the work he carried out."

Captain Johnnie Walker is profoundly deserving of this statue at Liverpool Pier Head, unveiled by Prince Philip in 2007, who himself was based at Western Approaches during the Battle of the Atlantic.

66 Victory has been won and shall be won by such as he. May there never be wanting in this realm a succession of men of like spirit and discipline, imagination and valour, humble and unafraid. All the sea of the Western Approaches shall be his tomb. 99

Admiral Horton, in his funeral eulogy to Capt Walker at Liverpool Cathedral

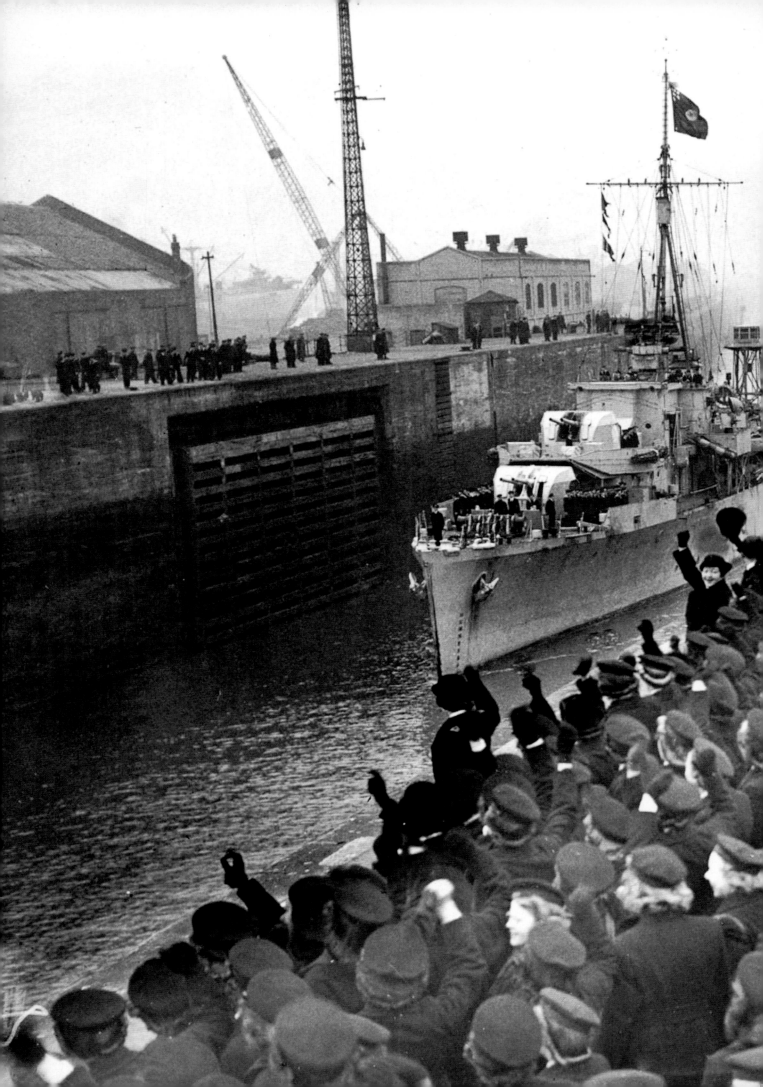

Captain Johnny Walker led the most successful anti-submarine patrol of the Atlantic in January 1944. The patrol – the 2nd Support Group – led by Walker's flagship HMS Starling, had already notched up an impressive five U-boat kills.

The Group set sail from Liverpool on January 29 to the strains of A Hunting we Will Go played over HMS Starling's loudspeakers. Walker's patrol claimed its first victim just two days later when U-592 was lost with all hands. Another four U-boats were to be sunk between February 8-11. The Group's next victim was on February 19 when U-264 was sent to the bottom, but this time the entire crew was saved.

The tally of six U-boats in 27 days was an incredible feat and, as shown, the Group was met by an ecstatic crowd of hundreds of people when it finally came home to Gladstone Dock.

Below, an old Liverpool Daily Post photo of captured U-boat Captain Kretschmer walking off HMS Walker onto Princes Landing Stage. It was on the night of 16 March 1941 when Captain Donald Macintyre's 5th Escort Group, led by the destroyer HMS Walker, defeated the German Wolf Pack attack on Convoy HX 122 south of Iceland. Otto Kretschmer was captured after his U-99 was forced to surface by depth charges from the Walker. Right, Captain Donald Macintyre

The end for Otto

CAPT Johnnie Walker and the 36th Escort and 2nd Support Groups formed only some of the protection, from both sides of the Atlantic, which was offered to merchant convoys.

Some of the less high-profile work was carried out by Capt Donald Macintyre, 5th Escort Group Commander, who fought through five years of the war.

In March 1941, Capt Macintyre, commanding HMS Walker, led the force which finally ended the career of U-boat ace Otto Kretschmer, who was landed at Liverpool and interned in the Preston North End football stadium.

As conflict moved on, Captain Macintyre patrolled the Atlantic at the head of Escort Group B2 where he chased the U-boats, and by 1944 he was in charge of a new type of anti-submarine ship, HMS Bickerton, leading 5th Escort Group. Unfortunately, Bickerton was later torpedoed.

Postwar, Capt Macintyre took up writing books about his experiences, including U-boat Killer and The Battle of the Atlantic.

A crucial element in the Battle of the Atlantic which must be emphasised is the vital role which the British Commonwealth played in eventually securing the Allied victory.

It is hard to imagine that Britain could have won the Battle of the Atlantic without the unflinching support of Canada and the Royal Canadian Navy.

Canada suffered its own casualties in protecting the convoys which interminably ploughed back and forth across the north Atlantic.

A German U-Boat sinks following an attack by destroyers and corvettes on convoy escort duty in 1941

Keeping a look out for U-boats on a convoy across the Atlantic

THE FIGHT FOR FREEDOM

LIVERPOOL handled at least one third of the country's imports and was the main terminus for Atlantic trade convoys.

A convoy arrived every other day in the Mersey, and during the war handled over 75 million tons of cargo.

Almost 74,000 aeroplanes and

gliders were also brought into the port. Often the cargo ships were like sitting ducks for fast German raiders and U-boats, but still on they came. Another attack beaten off. A rare moment of respite.

Canon Bob Evans, former head of the Mersey Mission to Seamen, said: "This part of the world was

the heartbeat of the survival of this country. Without our gentlemen and ladies, we would not have survived those dark years.

"Talking to an old seaman, I asked him what he remembered of the Battle of the Atlantic. He said it was the cries of men in the sea at night from sunken ships and we could

not stop to save them.

"Also, the stupid people at home grumbling about the lack of food when others were at sea."

In the Second World War, Britain was on the edge of survival, said Canon Evans.

"Winston Churchill said we were within two weeks of losing the war, but the ladies and gentlemen of Liverpool and elsewhere did it for this country."

Patrick Moran, chairman of Liverpool Retired Seafarers Association, who has organised many Battle of the Atlantic and Merchant Navy Remembrance Day events, said: "It is very important that people remember the sacrifice of ordinary seamen and women from Merseyside, the UK and Commonwealth.

"The Battle of the Atlantic is often forgotten. These commemoration events are a means of not forgetting the courage of those no longer with us."

On patrol in the Atlantic. Below, maps show the main convoy routes and ships sunk during 1943 and 1944

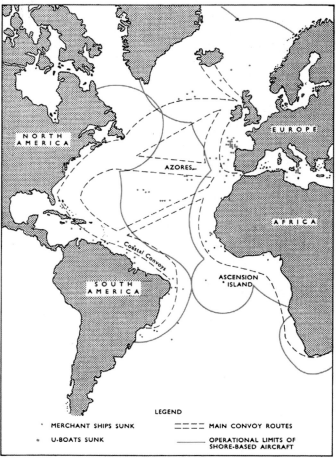

June – August 1943

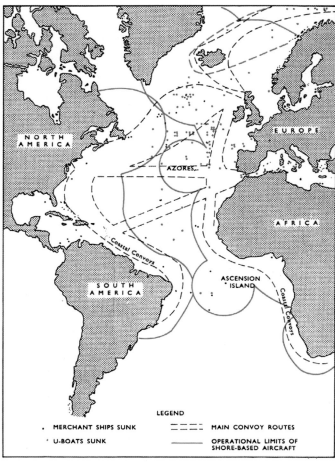

September 1943 – April 1944

Above, a commander and pilot officer on bridge of a destroyer, 1941. Below, a convoy of steamers, pictured astern, June 1942

A minesweeper in WW II convoy, 1945

A short Sunderland Flying Boat of the RAF Coastal Command patrols above an Atlantic convoy 500 miles south west of Ireland

Life aboard a Royal Navy corvette escorting a convoy across the Atlantic at the height of the U-boat offensive against in August 1942, with the depth charges arrayed around the stern of the ship

Allied tanker torpedoed in the Atlantic Ocean by German submarine in 1942

An oil tanker ablaze after being torpedoed by a German U-boat in the North Atlantic, July 1940. Left, Royal Navy sailors aboard a destroyer on escort duty, May 1940

Rolling nicely in the Westerlies

> **"The sea was in our blood, and our blood was in the sea, and that's enough about those five martial years, which made a man out of me and a corpse out of my brother."**

The Cruel Sea

NICHOLAS Monsarrat's seminal evocation of the Battle of the Atlantic, in his best-seller The Cruel Sea, in 1951, is regarded as the definitive novel of the conflict and became a hugely successful film.

Born in 1910, the son of a leading Liverpool surgeon, the young Nicholas Monsarrat lived in Rodney Street and was inspired to write by the sight of a plaque dedicated to the poet Arthur Hughes Clough on a neighbouring house.

During summers at the Monsarrats' country home on Anglesey, the young Nicholas' love of the sea and sailing blossomed. These sailing skills later enabled him to join the Royal Naval Volunteer Reserve in 1940, after seeing an advertisement for "gentlemen with yachting experience".

As an RNVR officer, based in Albert Dock, he was in the thick of the Battle, sailing the North Atlantic in the most ferocious and unforgiving times for three years aboard Flower-class escort corvettes, described as "unglamorous bath-tubs armed with popguns".

These were ships which were so unstable on the high seas, that sailors joked they "would roll on wet grass".

Yet they were the tough little warships charged with shepherding the vital convoys through the marauding U-boat wolf packs.

One of his most bizarre and lucky escapes was in Liverpool itself when, 24 hours after his ship, HMS Campanula, sailed from Albert Dock, a dormant land-mine lying beneath her berth exploded.

Between the watches he kept a diary of life aboard: true tales of heroism, fear and frequently death. Later on he commanded a frigate.

He caused a great sensation with three books published during the war, collected together in 1945 as Three Corvettes, stories that were in essence a prelude to his magnum opus, The Cruel Sea.

"Nicholas Monsarrat was a perceptive writer who experienced the extremes of warfare with both its action and monotony," said the late Prof Quentin Hughes, of Merseyside Civic Society.

"He encapsulates the whole spirit of the Battle of the Atlantic in several novels in a way that no ordinary reporting could convey."

These books brought home to people what it was really like to be in the conflict through Monsarrat's fiction distilled from his brutal, first-hand experience.

Nicholas Monsarrat died in 1979, aged 69, and his nephew Giles recalled: "I went to Portsmouth for his burial at sea by the Royal Navy aboard HMS Scylla. We sailed into The Solent and stood on the quarterdeck as his ashes were scattered overboard.

"My mum Felicity asked if any of the crew had read The Cruel Sea and was told 'We've all read The Cruel Sea'. She was very pleased, as she was so proud of her brother."

THE COST OF WAR

By 1945 around 12,600 Mersey seafarers had lost their lives in the Battle of the Atlantic.

Liverpool ship-owners had lost more than three million tons of shipping, mostly in the Atlantic. This is the equivalent to losing 630 ships of 5,000 gross tons each, or a quarter of all UK merchant ship losses (12.5 million gross tons). Liverpool ship-owners alone lost three quarters of their merchant tonnage. This was more than the entire Merchant Navy tonnages of Norway (two million tons), Netherlands (one and half million tons) and Greece (one million tons).

A total of 36,000 Allied Merchant Seamen were killed in the Battle of the Atlantic, plus 36,200 Allied Naval personnel. Almost 6,000 members of RAF Coastal Command were lost.

Out of the 3,150 convoys, more than 2,800 Allied merchant ships were sunk (15 million tons) and 175 warships lost.

Canada's Merchant Navy was vital to the Allied cause during World War II. More than 70 Canadian merchant vessels were lost. 1,600 merchant sailors were killed, including eight women.

The German U-boat fleet totalled 1,157 U-boats of which 789 were lost. Some 30,000 German submariners were killed, which was 75 per cent of the total force. The Axis (Germany and Italy) powers also lost most of its 700 midget submarines.

German battle cruiser Admiral Von Hipper bombs HMS Glowworm, April 6, 1940

THE LACONIA

One Liverpool liner gave her name to a command issued by none other than Admiral Karl Doenitz, chief of the German Kriegsmarine.

The "Laconia Order" came into being after an abortive U-boat rescue attempt during the Battle of the Atlantic, as graphically depicted in a recent television drama by Liverpool playwright Alan Bleasdale.

Following the liner's trademark smoky trail, U-156 commanded by Kapitanleutnant Werner Hartenstein, torpedoed Laconia off West Africa on September 12, 1942.

Laconia was carrying 2,732 crew, passengers, soldiers, including hundreds of POWs from Italy, then a German ally. On surfacing, Hartenstein and his crew immediately started a rescue and were joined by the crews of other U-boats in the area. Laconia's master Capt Rudolph Sharp, who survived Lancastria's sinking went down with his ship.

While attempting a rendezvous with French warships and displaying Red Cross banners, the U-boats, packed with survivors inside and on their outside decks, were attacked by a US Army Liberator bomber.

Hence Doenitz's "Laconia Order" to stop rescuing civilian survivors and ushering in the Kriegsmarine's unrestricted submarine warfare. The moral dilemma over the Laconia incident, about whether military forces should give assistance and protection to non-combatants at sea during wartime is at the heart of Bleasdale's screenplay.

CITY OF BENARES

One of the most heart-rending wartime stories from the Battle of the Atlantic concerns the loss of the Liverpool liner City of Benares.

Aboard this fine Ellerman City Line steamship were 100 children, whose parents believed sending their youngsters on a government-backed scheme to Canada was for the best at a time when the German Blitz raged and invasion was a constant threat.

With 407 people aboard, SS City of Benares sailed from Liverpool for Quebec and Montreal, on September 13, 1940, as the leader on the 19-ship convoy OB213. Four days later, the convoy escort warships redeployed to an in-bound convoy. Just hours later at 10.30pm in a fierce thunder storm, City of Benares was spotted and torpedoed by U-48.

The resulting explosion ripped through liner's engineroom and she sank by the stern in 15 minutes. Amid the terrifying conditions aboard, the pyjama-clad children had to leave their cabin bunks and find their way on deck and into lifeboats.

Not all lifeboats were launched successfully and others were swamped by huge waves. Other survivors sat waist deep in water and perished through exposure. Only 158 people survived and more than 250 people perished in a force 8 gale.

When the Liverpool-based destroyer HMS Hurricane arrived the following day, some of the survivors crippled by shock and hypothermia were unable to climb aboard unaided.

Unfortunately lifeboat 12 was unaccounted for and drifted for eight days with only a week's water supply for the 40 people aboard, including six children. Luckily, those who survived this second ordeal, were spotted by an aircraft and rescued by HMS Anthony.

Blake Simms, whose father Capt Hugh Crofton Simms commanded HMS Hurricane, was keen that the tragedy must be remembered and tracked down survivors for reunions

He befriended the remaining youngest survivors, particularly Bess Cummings, and Beth Williams, the only Liverpool girl to survive the sinking, who later married Bess' brother Geoff. Beth, originally from Orrell Park, who now lives in Yorkshire, said: "We went to bed that night at 6pm.

"The next thing we were woken by an almighty explosion. I knew immediately we had been torpedoed. "All the lights had gone out and the smell of sulphur was overpowering."

Of the 100 children aboard, Beth was just one of 13 left. The government immediately abandoned the evacuation programme.

The attack came during a period of the Second World War dubbed "the Happy Time". The fall of France in June 1940 permitted the Germans to use the French Atlantic ports as U-boat bases allowing them to range in unrestricted warfare far out into the Atlantic and the Mediterranean for the first time.

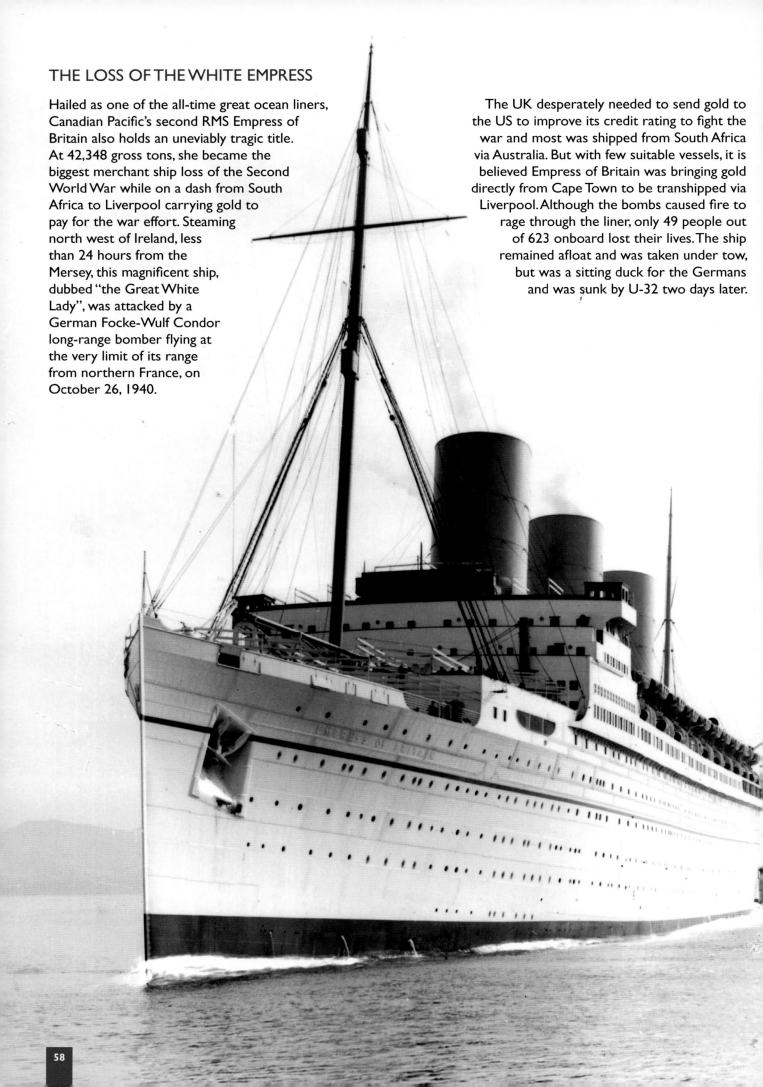

THE LOSS OF THE WHITE EMPRESS

Hailed as one of the all-time great ocean liners, Canadian Pacific's second RMS Empress of Britain also holds an uneviably tragic title. At 42,348 gross tons, she became the biggest merchant ship loss of the Second World War while on a dash from South Africa to Liverpool carrying gold to pay for the war effort. Steaming north west of Ireland, less than 24 hours from the Mersey, this magnificent ship, dubbed "the Great White Lady", was attacked by a German Focke-Wulf Condor long-range bomber flying at the very limit of its range from northern France, on October 26, 1940.

The UK desperately needed to send gold to the US to improve its credit rating to fight the war and most was shipped from South Africa via Australia. But with few suitable vessels, it is believed Empress of Britain was bringing gold directly from Cape Town to be transhipped via Liverpool. Although the bombs caused fire to rage through the liner, only 49 people out of 623 onboard lost their lives. The ship remained afloat and was taken under tow, but was a sitting duck for the Germans and was sunk by U-32 two days later.

FORGOTTEN TRAGEDY OF LIVERPOOL SHIPPING

John Sawyer pictured on the Lancastria in 1935

Britain's worst maritime disaster was the loss of Liverpool's Lancastria in the Battle of the Atlantic

RMS LANCASTRIA, one of Cunard Line's pre-war premier cruise liners has the infamous claim to being one of top three merchantmen disasters of all time and Britain's biggest maritime disaster.

With at least 4,000 people killed, it also the highest death toll for UK forces in a single engagement in the entire Second World War.

A tragedy so overwhelming that Prime Minister Winston Churchill, fearing the effect on morale after Dunkirk, decided it was too unbearable to be reported. He never lifted the ban.

Maybe up to 7,000 souls were packed aboard the Liverpool-based liner, as she was about to depart from her anchorage off St Nazaire, as France fell in the Second World War.

Lancastria was part of Operation Aerial, a near-forgotten mop-up mission to evacuate the 150,000 soldiers left behind in Europe after Dunkirk. Troops and refugees fled into St Nazaire ahead of the German advance through France.

Capt Rudolph Sharp, of Birkenhead, delayed Lancastria's departure on June 17, 1940, hoping for an armed escort down the Loire estuary to scare off U-boats lurking off-shore. Then a Junkers Ju88 dive-bomber squadron scored four direct hits, which smashed through cargo holds (packed with airmen) and down the funnel (or near it). Lancastria turned turtle, with people scrambling for their lives and thick fuel oil coating everyone black.

Survivors rescued by British destroyers were officially ordered not to talk about the tragedy on arrival in Plymouth.

The immediate aftermath was recalled by John Sawyer, a former Cunard Line QE2 executive hotel manager, from West Kirby, who started his sea-going career on Lancastria, aged 14, as a bell-boy, 1935.

He was aboard the next Cunard liner, Franconia, to follow Lancastria into St Nazaire.and recalled: "We knew that Lancastria had gone down that afternoon. We were dive-bombed as we approached the harbour and the shock waves from several near-misses put our engines out of action.

"There were 127 ships around us in Quiberon Bay. Next morning they had all gone. Our engineers worked up to their necks in water trying to get things going.

"At 10am a British destroyer pulled alongside and hailed us, saying, 'The position is out of hand. Goodbye and good luck'. We could see gun fire in the distance. Then, suddenly at 1pm, Franconia began moving and we limped back to Liverpool at five knots."

Poor Capt Sharp, rescued from the Lancastria, later transferred to the Laconia, which was torpedoed off Freetown, West Africa. This became the second greatest British WWII merchant loss, with at least 1,641 souls dead including her captain.

In wartime's black humour, John Sawyer remembered Capt Sharp was nicknamed "the Nazi" among Cunard crews, because he lost two big British liners thereby inadvertently aiding Germany's war effort.

The Liverpool Escort Group was made famous by the successful patrols under the command of Captain Johnny Walker. H-class destroyer HMS Hotspur enters the Mersey from Gladstone Dock for another Western Approaches sortie to guard the vital convoys

FROM THE BANKS OF THE MERSEY

Night and day, the sheds of the old yard down by the banks of the Mersey, throbbed to the sounds of men building the ships which would help the Allies beat the Germans.

EVEN as one of Britain's major shipyards and specialists in warship construction, Cammell Laird exceeded its own high standards during the Second World War.

It built 106 naval vessels during the conflict, with an astonishing average of one ship every 21 days. Besides newbuilds, yard's largest ever workforce of 12,000 men also completed repairs on 2,000 merchant vessels and 120 warships, including nine battleships and 11 aircraft carriers.

John Syvret, Cammell Laird current chief executive, said: "Just before the outbreak of war Cammell Laird launched the Ark Royal, the first Royal Navy vessel designed and built as an aircraft carrier. Significantly one of HMS Ark Royal's first missions in 1939 was to the South Atlantic on a search for the German heavy cruiser Graf Spee.

"She also played a key role together with the Cammell Laird battleship HMS Prince of Wales in sinking the Bismarck in the North Atlantic in May 1941, before she

HMS Rodney fires her secondary armament of six inch guns during exercises at sea in December 1940

was later torpedoed by a U-Boat in November 1941 near Gibraltar.

"Meanwhile, HMS Prince of Wales later took the Prime Minister Winston Churchill to Newfoundland to meet President Roosevelt to discuss the Atlantic Charter, before being sunk by Japanese torpedo bombers off Malaya with the loss of 307 lives in December 1941."

In 1927, Cammell Laird built HMS Rodney, one of the two most powerful battleships afloat, which

also played a major role in the sinking of the German battleship Bismarck.

Another Cammell Laird battleship, HMS Royal Oak, was anchored at the supposedly safe haven of Scapa Flow in Orkney when she was torpedoed on October 14, 1939, by U-47, commanded by Günther Prien.

Tragically 833 men died out of Royal Oak's 1,234 crew, and the event badly damaged national morale at the war's beginning.

With her motto, Non Generat Aquilae Columbas (Eagles Do Not Breed Doves), Rodney was the eighth Royal Navy battleship to carry the name. She was built in Birkenhead and launched in 1928. At 38,000 tons and fitted with 16-inch guns, she was a formidable vessel, whose greatest moment came in the campaign to destroy the Bismarck 1941.

The British Government had been profoundly shaken by the Battle of Denmark Strait of May 24 in which Prince of Wales and our largest ship, HMS Hood, engaged Prinz Eugen off the coast of Iceland. Hood was sunk with only three of her crew of 1,400 surviving. Prince of Wales suffered some damage. The Senior Service needed revenge and it came on May 26 when Bismarck, by now separated from Prinz Eugen, was spotted about 700 miles off Brest, France. Her rudders were jammed after successful attacks by Ark Royal's Swordfish torpedo planes.

That night, Rodney and King George V arrived and the following morning pounded the crippled Bismarck with their heavy guns for 90 minutes.

By then "a flaming shambles" she was finished off with three torpedoes and sank at 10.36am.

Thus, Birkenhead ships had played the leading roles in one of Britain's first victories of the war.

Above, Bismarck Survivors alongside HMS Dorsetshire, May 27, 1941. Bottom photograph, a British fleet consisting of Battleships HMS Rodney, HMS Resolution, HMS Royal Oak and HMS Royal Sovereign and battlecruiser HMS Repulse, August 1939

A squadron of Fairey Swordfish planes on board HMS Ark Royal prepare to launch from the flight deck

Regarded as such a symbol of British maritime might, the Germans falsely reported several times sinking HMS Ark Royal, the Royal Navy's most advanced aircraft carrier.

Ark Royal was involved in practically every major naval campaign during the war's first two years and many enduring carrier techniques were perfected on her decks.

On September 14, 1939, planes from Ark Royal scored the first Allied victory against the German submarine fleet by sinking U-39 off NW Ireland.

With the battleship Renown, she also hunted for the German pocket battleship Graf Spee in the South Atlantic.

Joining the famous Force H, Ark Royal took part in Operation Catapult to neutralize the French fleet in Algeria, in which her Swordfish aircraft sank the battlecruiser Dunkerque. Italy's declaration of war on June 10, 1940, endangered British naval supply lines to Egypt and especially Malta, midway between Gibraltar and Alexandria.

Ark Royal was deployed on many operations against Italian air raids from Cagliari, Sardinia. In September she failed in an attempt to land General de Gaulle's Free French forces at Senegal. After several weeks' repair at Birkenhead, she headed back to attack Cagliari and then took part in the Battle

of Spartivento. In spring 1941 she made regular runs to Malta delivering Hurricane fighters to the beleaguered island. With Force H, Ark Royal was deployed to search for Bismarck and on the morning of May 26, 1941, 10 of her Swordfishes flew off her decks (pitching some 50ft in high winds and sea), sighting the great German battleship at 11.15am. That night, Ark Royal's planes scored the crucial two hits that knocked out Bismarck's steering gear. While back on duty dedicated to the relief of Malta, on November 13, Ark Royal was torpedoed by U-81, 30 miles off Gibraltar and the next morning she sank with the loss of only one life.

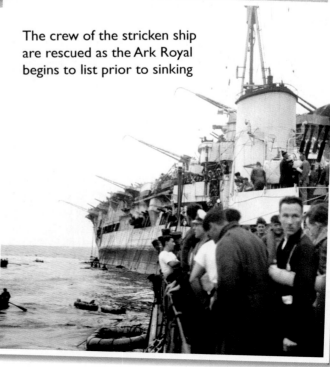

The crew of the stricken ship are rescued as the Ark Royal begins to list prior to sinking

Before being sunk by Japanese dive-bombers in the South China Sea, the Birkenhead-built battleship, HMS Prince of Wales, had a short but illustrious career of less than a year.

In August, 1941, Prime Minister Winston Churchill took a hazardous transatlantic voyage aboard HMS Prince of Wales, which was only completed by Cammell Laird in March 1941.

His destination was Placentia Bay, Canada, and his mission was to meet US President Franklin D Roosevelt, ostensibly to agree the Atlantic Charter outlining the ideology for a postwar world and international security.

However, there were other motivations at the meetings aboard USS Augusta on August 9-14, 1941. The US had not yet entered the war, so Roosevelt was also attempting to tie Britain to concrete war aims and Churchill was desperate to bring the US into the war effort. The US entered the war on December 7, 1941, after the Japanese attack on Pearl Harbour.

Above, HMS Prince of Wales at Argentia, Newfoundland, August 1941. After escorting Winston Churchill across the Atlantic, Prince of Wales successfully engaged Italian planes off Malta in late September, before she steamed to the Pacific. When the Japanese landed in Malaya on December 7 – the day of the Pearl Harbor raid – Prince of Wales and the battle-cruiser HMS Repulse (pictured right) were sent fruitlessly to attack the invaders. On December 10, while returning to Singapore, the warships were attacked by Japanese bombers and torpedo planes. With no air defence, they were both sunk. These were the first British capital ships to be destroyed by air attack at sea and added to the international shock reverberating over Pearl Harbor.

HMS Prince of Wales arriving at Singapore December, 1941

Pivotal to the campaign against the U-boats was the work of the Special Support Groups, composed of escort vessels such as corvettes, frigates and destroyers. One of the most famous and successful of these groups was that based in Liverpool's Gladstone Dock, which was used as a base for the many warships. Below, H-class destroyer HMS Hesperus arrives at Gladstone Dock December 1942, with damage to the bow after ramming and sinking U-357

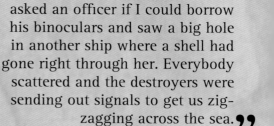

"Four days out in the Atlantic we were torpedoed twice. Lowering the lifeboat we got hit by the second torpedo. I was knocked out of the lifeboat. While I was being washed away, the U-boat surfaced near me and I got hold of a small iron rung. I looked up and the conning tower opened up – three or four Germans stood there scanning the ocean. They saw me so I shouted for help, but they closed the hatch and started moving away. Then I let go and the lifeboat picked me up."

Sidney McConville, of Croxteth, crew on Dutch ship MV Abberk, sailing Trinidad – Liverpool

> We would sail, always in strict black-out, in convoy – often 60 ships, all heavily loaded, often with only one or two escorts. Ships in the middle bore black flags as they were carrying TNT. The Royal Navy was excellent but greatly overworked. I crossed the North Atlantic about 20 times, often from Halifax, Nova Scotia, and once or twice from West Africa. We often crossed in winter, as far north as Greenland. There were a lot of icebergs and you would get as close to the ice edge as you could . It was a deterrent, but we still had U-boat raids. It often took 17-20 days to cross. I never saw a man leave his post and they ranged from 14-70 years old. Being at sea in those days was like being in jail, with a damn good chance of being drowned.

Jack Brotheridge, of Crosby

> The Atlantic is a very formidable ocean, a very cruel sea, but it held a special fascination to the men and women of Merseyside and beyond. We were a bunch of people, flung together under extreme circumstances, never knowing what was going to happen next. But following the code of the sea, like the many thousands who had gone before, we signed on and did our bit, come what may.

Henry Savage, merchant seaman

VICTORY ON THE HORIZON

> **"The Battle of the Atlantic was not won by any navy or air force, it was won by the courage, fortitude and determination of the British and Allied Merchant Navy."**
>
> *Rear Admiral Leonard Murray, Commander-in-Chief, Canadian North Atlantic, Royal Canadian Navy*

Clockwise from top left; Obersteurmann Helmut Klotzch yells for help after his submarine, U-175, is sunk in the Atlantic in April 1943; a rare picture taken from a Canadian Corvette showing a German U-Boat making an effort to escape after being rammed during a surface fight in 1942; a German U-boat caught in a hail of gunfire and bombs in the Bay of Biscay, June 1942

Guarding our convoys – men aboard a destroyer
on escort duty fire warning shots to unidentified
aircraft by 2-pounder Pom Pom, April 1940

British destroyers sink a U-boat in August 1940

Hitler's U-boat wolf packs are towed six to eight at a time from Loch Ryan to a 'graveyard' off the Bloody Foreland, North West Ireland, as part of Operation Deadlight

Race against time to crack the Enigma code

WHILE the mariners fought in the cold waters of the Atlantic, back at home the boffins had a battle of their own on their hands. Mathematicians fought to crack the German Navy Enigma code, which was one of the most difficult to break.

The complex Enigma cipher machine encrypted messages using a series of rotors, plug boards and code books. Codes and the rotor settings changed regularly.

It directed German U-boats and naval craft around the Atlantic where they struck at Allied shipping, crippling Britain's crucial supply links with the outside world.

The Admiralty ordered a series of lightning strikes against German shipping with the specific aim of capturing Enigma machines and their code books. The attacks had to be a complete surprise so German crews did not destroy documents and tip the machines overboard.

Between April 1941 and June 1944, five raids were carried out. At least two Enigma machines and a host of documents and code books were captured. As a result, experts at Bletchley Park broke the code and Allied shipping losses, which had peaked in 1942, started to fall.

In January and February 1943

alone they were halved. Breaking the code helped the Allies to locate U-boat positions and move convoys around them, while attacking with U-boat destroyers.

The Germans never really understood why, by May 1943, the tide had turned.

Some 42 surrendered U-boats at Lisahally, Lough Foyle, near Londonderry, Northern Ireland

66 The Germans never really understood why, by May 1943, the tide had turned. 99

> **"The Battle of the Atlantic was the dominating factor all through the war. Never for one moment could we forget that everything happening elsewhere, on land, at sea or in the air depended ultimately on its outcome."**
> *Winston Churchill*

World War II Prime Minister Winston Churchill visiting Liverpool in June 1945, in Lime Street, with The Vines Hotel, right